BRAVE AND BRILLIANT
The Secrets To Making An Impact, Leaving A Legacy And Inspiring Cultural Shift

For permission requests, speaking inquiries, bulk orders, and purchase options, email hello@izdiharjamil.com.

Interior, Cover, Layout, and Graphic Design
Dr. Hanim Romainoor, Ph.D. and Dr. Izdihar Jamil, Ph.D.

Produced by Diamond Queen, LLC
Edited by Hallie Guidry

Disclaimer:
The authors in no way, shape, or form consider any of the information in this book to be advice, promise, guarantee, warranty, or any form of professional advice. It is intended for informational and educational purposes only. The results produced by the authors, or anyone referenced in the book, are mentioned for illustration purposes only and are not intended to imply or suggest that you will have results that are at all similar to those in the book.

ISBN: 979-8-9897865-9-6 (Paperback)
ISBN: 979-8-9897865-8-9 (EPUB)

BRAVE AND BRILLIANT

THE SECRETS TO MAKING AN IMPACT,
LEAVING A LEGACY AND INSPIRING
CULTURAL SHIFT

Featuring

BOLD SPEAKERS
From Diverse Backgrounds

BARRIERS

I know you're looking at me
But do you really see me?
Are you threatened?
Am I suspicious?
Because I look different

I know you're probably judging me
But these Whispers are misleading

I feel a shaking in my bones
See your Eyes cold as stone
If I run … will it ever change?

Barriers … Barriers
Pushing through barriers
I gotta change the way I see you
If you're ever gonna see me

Barriers … Barriers
Pushing through barriers
We gotta love a little harder
We gotta hold each other stronger

I know you don't hear your words
Or the way that they hurt
As they're playing
Over and over and over again in my mind…

As my children find me
Laying on the floor
Tears streaming down my face
Trying to open up my heart to you

Barriers … Barriers
Pushing through barriers
I gotta change the way I see you
If you're ever gonna see me

Barriers … Barriers
Pushing through barriers
We gotta love a little harder
We gotta hold each other stronger

Can we find the footsteps in the dark
To where there's nothing but love

Barriers … Barriers
Pushing through barriers
I got to change the way I see you
If you're ever gonna see me

Barriers … Barriers
Pushing through barriers
We gotta love a little harder
We gotta hold each other stronger

Pushing through barriers
Pushing through barriers

Breaking down barriers
Breaking down barriers

Music written by Izdihar Jamil and Drew Lawrence
Music composed by Drew Lawrence
Sung by Izdihar Jamil

To hear the song, go to:
https://www.izdiharjamil.com/songs

Table of Contents

Barriers ii

Table of Contents v

Introduction 1

CHAPTER 1
Dr. Izdihar Jamil, Ph.D.
Take The Leap 7

CHAPTER 2
Carol Barkes, CPM
Extinguishing the Flames of Conflict 18

CHAPTER 3
Cindy Warden
Success Is For Losers 26

CHAPTER 4
Dr. Danielle Zanzarov, Ph.D.
The Bravest Action You Can Take 35

CHAPTER 5
Diego Perez
A Heart in Waiting 45

CHAPTER 6
Hannah Kim
What Performing in Prisons Taught Me 50

CHAPTER 7

Captain Jeremy Stoker

Inside the Cockpit: Prioritize Like a Pilot *59*

CHAPTER 8

Ruben Perez

Jern-e: My AI Co-Pilot *69*

Conclusion 78

8 Tips to Be Brave and Brilliant 78

BONUS: The Guidelines 83

Introduction

I was on a Zoom call at my home office in Orange County when my client Michelle said, "Izzy, you've got to speak on the TEDx stage." It's been one of my dreams for many years, but I said. "I just had a baby, and I'm scared of public speaking. I don't think I can do that."

Then Michelle said, "You're a trailblazer. Where you go, people follow. You want to create a path so other people can follow."

Many thoughts and emotions came through me. Can I really do it? How will I manage speaking on the TEDx stage and caring for a baby? Public speaking just scares me—why do I even want to put myself through that torture?

It's just too much work.

But then I said, "Okay, let's do it." I applied to the first TEDx conference, and the next one, and the next one. Multiple organizers said 'NO' to me back-to-back. By the ninth organizer who said 'NO,' I picked up the phone, called Michelle, and said, "They said 'NO.'" I cried because when you get rejected by your dreams, it hurts.

There were times when I said to myself, "What's the point of doing this? It's just easier for me to give up." A few days later, as I was scrolling through Facebook, I saw a post by Michelle. She shared that TEDxDelthroneWomen was looking for speakers. I felt a sensation in my body, but I didn't know what it was. It was as if my body was directing me to explore more about this event.

I checked them out, and I looked at their website and social media. The event was precisely what I was looking for. I wanted to speak at an event that showcased diverse and powerful women. I also wanted it to be within an hour's drive from home because I was still nursing Rayhan. I reached out to the organizer, Sonali Fiske. I said hello and asked about her vision and theme for the event. She said that the theme was "REVOLUTION."

As I was filling out the application, I really, really wanted to say this message, but I was flooded with the thoughts, "Don't do it. It'll be too much. They're not going to like it. It's too bold." Then another thought came into my mind, "The theme is REVOLUTION. Play BIG."

I made a decision to be brave and bold; then I gave myself permission to express myself. After all, revolution doesn't happen when you're being timid or hiding. So, I wrote down on the application, "It takes BALLS to wear the hijab in America," said a prayer, and sent it. A few weeks later, I received an email from Sonali. She said, "Congratulations, you've been accepted as a speaker at TEDxDelthroneWomen." It was a good fit for both of us because our visions were in alignment with each other.

On December 4th, 2021, I gave my TEDx talk "Coming to America: A Story of a Hijab-Wearing Woman" sharing my idea of how to overcome social adversity as an immigrant and hijab-wearing Muslim woman.

Since then, I've received messages from people all around the world telling me how my talk has inspired them to be brave, embrace who they are, and make bold decisions that are not tied to society's rules. I've seen how my talk has impacted not only my family and friends, but my community and society and, hopefully, will continue to do so for many years to come.

One of the biggest reasons that I decided to curate and organize a TEDx event is to create a platform, a vessel for the voices of my community to be heard and understood. There were many challenges that I had to overcome, but the reward, impact, and lessons learned are beyond valuable. I am very grateful to be the vessel in creating a movement within my community and hopefully leave a meaningful legacy for our children.

The book "BRAVE AND BRILLIANT" is a culmination of unique ideas from the authors who are also speakers at TEDxHuntingtonBeach 2024. Their intention is simple: to share their voices in impacting the community to be brave and brilliant using their own unique perspectives.

It has been such a joy to curate this book and hopefully, it'll serve as your guide to creating a life of BRAVE AND BRILLIANT POSSIBILITIES. Here's an overview of what each author contributed to this book.

Dr. Izdihar Jamil, Ph.D., reminds us to "Take The Leap." When things don't go as planned, letting go and surrendering can create space for the best things or people to come our way. We are vessels for a greater plan, and adjustments are part of fulfilling a higher vision.

Carol Barkes, in "Extinguishing the Flames of Conflict," teaches us the value of trying unconventional approaches. Being "conflict curious" means looking at situations with curiosity instead of judgment, helping us resolve conflicts more effectively.

Cindy Warden, in "Success Is For Losers," shares her journey of inner transformation. She emphasizes letting go of limiting beliefs to achieve a more authentic and fulfilling version of success. While success is often viewed as adding "MORE" to your credentials, Cindy invites you to lose it all.

Dr. Danielle Zanzarov, Ph.D., in "The Bravest Action You Can Take," invites us to be brave by disconnecting from distractions and connecting with our inner selves. This connection helps us make conscious and impactful decisions.

Diego Perez, in "A Heart In Waiting," emphasizes the profound impact of embracing vulnerability and taking bold steps into the unknown. He reflects on moments when fear nearly held him back, but choosing courage led to personal growth and unforgettable experiences. His journey from running a marathon at 16 to delivering a TED talk showcases how stepping outside our comfort zones can transform our lives.

Hannah Kim, in "What Performing in Prisons Taught Me," highlights the power of vulnerability and emotional transparency in performance. This approach can breach even the hardest hearts, creating profound connections and transformations.

Captain Jeremy Stoker, in "Inside the Cockpit: Prioritize Like a Pilot," shares three priorities: Aviate, Navigate, and Communicate. These principles help manage and strategize during critical situations.

Ruben Perez, in "Jern-e: My AI Co-Pilot," encourages us to embrace AI as a collaborator that amplifies our human potential. By blending creativity, intuition, and emotional intelligence with AI, we can push the boundaries of what's possible.

The book ends with a chapter that culminates with the key idea of how you can make an impact, leave a legacy, and inspire a cultural shift in "8 Tips To Be Brave and Brilliant."

There is also a BONUS chapter with practical tips and guidelines to land your dream TEDx talk by the team members of TEDxHuntingtonBeach 2024. We would love for you to share your unique idea on the coveted red dot!

Our wish is for you to enjoy reading this book, take appropriate and relatable tips from it, and turn them into meaningful actions.

Be open and accepting of each other's differences and take brave actions to stand in your greatness.

Best Wishes,
Izdihar
Visibility Expert | TEDx Curator | Bestselling Author
https://www.izdiharjamil.com/

1

Take The Leap

Dr. Izdihar Jamil, Ph.D.
Author | TEDx Curator | Visibility Expert

"In my moment of loneliness and uncertainty, I decided that I was enough and that I was capable of handling things with love, compassion, and wisdom." – Dr. Izdihar Jamil

The Red Dot

On December 4, 2021, I stood on the coveted red dot on the TEDxDelthroneWomen stage near Los Angeles, giving my TEDx talk, "Coming to America: A Story of a Hijab-Wearing Woman," a dream of mine for many years. In front of me were about one hundred audience members. The venue was dark; I could only see the front row, but I knew there were more rows behind them. In front of me were three camera crew members, one on the left, right, and center of the stage.

I looked at a lady with long dark hair in the back row of the audience. She looked like Nadrah, my 9-year-old daughter. I directed my last sentence to her, imagining she was my daughter, "Be proud and courageous of our roots and heritage." I wanted Nadrah to always remember her roots as a Muslim woman and be brave within them. The audience almost instantly stood up and gave me one of the longest and loudest standing ovations of the day. I could see their faces: some with tears, some with smiles, and some with stoic expressions. I took a moment to absorb the audience's reaction, then I said, "Thank you," and walked off the stage.

After my talk, many people came up to me and said, "I wish my daughter was here to hear your story!" "I love your story, and what a beautiful message!" "You did an amazing job." I was deeply touched by how my story of coming to America and facing adversity resonated with others. From dealing with a bag of dog waste left on my doorstep to a neighbor calling the cops because of Nadrah's tantrum, these challenges highlighted my journey. It showed how I learned to be a proud Muslim woman, without conforming to society's expectations, and it was creating awareness in the community.

But one thing was on my mind that was diminishing the months of hard work and practice, robbing the joy and impact I was making. Somewhere during the talk, I froze and literally forgot my lines. The thoughts, "I forgot my lines. I screwed up. I messed up!" kept creeping back over and over again. Despite my best efforts and the positive encouragement I received, I walked home feeling guilty, ashamed, and exhausted.

The Fall Out

Following my TEDx talk, I received numerous messages from people around the world, saying how my talk touched their hearts and inspired them to be brave with their actions. This was beyond my imagination, seeing the rippling effects my idea could have on the community. What also surprised me was my burning desire to host a TEDx talk in my area. I felt an urge to create a platform to share my community's voices and provide unique solutions to their problems. I applied to become a licensee to host a TEDx event and a couple of weeks before Christmas, I received the news that my license for TEDxHuntingtonBeach was approved.

One of the first things I did when curating TEDxHuntingtonBeach was build a team around me. I knew I couldn't do this on my own and started strong with what I felt were good team members. I was in my home office in Orange County, and we were about to review the speaker applications when one of my team members said that she couldn't perform her task due to family circumstances. Although I understood her family commitment, I was relying on her to help filter through the applications and bounce ideas about choosing the speakers. Suddenly, I was left with a huge and heavy task alone. Then, two other team members fell out because of personal circumstances, and I was back to square one.

When I told my coach, Jeffrey, about the incidents, feeling bitter and let down, he said, "Think about it this way. When you started, you started on your own, and when the team members pulled out, you were still on your own. You actually didn't lose or gain anything, but you always had yourself." In my moment of loneliness and uncertainty, I decided that I was enough and that I was capable of handling things with love, compassion, and wisdom. I trusted that letting go of those team members early on was no indication of my capabilities but rather created a space for something or someone better.

A few weeks later, I went to Abrar's, my son's, hockey game and met another mom, Erin, at the freezing ice rink in Lakewood. We asked each other, "Which one is your kid?" and it turned out that our kids were on the same team. Most of our interaction was cheering and screaming for our kids during their games. Then, we started to share about what we do, and Erin asked for my TEDx talk because she said she loves TED talks.

When Erin mentioned that she was taking a mini-retirement from her corporate job, I mustered up a mountain of courage and asked her if she wanted to help me organize a TEDx event. I was prepared for her to say 'no' because I thought she would want to take it easy during her break, but she actually said 'YES!' It turned out that Erin was the perfect fit to be a team member for TEDxHuntingtonBeach. Her commitment and persistence made so many things possible, including a sold-out and successful inaugural event for TEDxHuntingtonBeach.

Show Time

We were at Talbert Middle School's theater on September 23, 2023, the day of the event for TEDxHuntingtonBeach. It was 2 p.m., and it was time to start, but the hall was half full despite the sold-out tickets. Erin said we couldn't start yet because we wanted to wait for the room to be three-quarters full to give the speakers and audience a great experience. Not only were we starting late, but there were also many empty seats!

I could see the speakers getting antsy and nervous— some of them were walking around, pacing, and meditating. When the theater was finally full, 30 minutes behind schedule, I walked onto the stage, smiling at the audience, and said, "My friend Michelle said, 'Izzy, you gotta speak on the TEDx stage.'" I then introduced the first-ever speaker of TEDxHuntingtonBeach, Drew Lawrence, an award-winning singer and songwriter.

As I stood in a dark corner opposite the stage, trying to breathe through unexpected back pain, I watched speaker after speaker grace the stage, standing on the red dot, giving everything they had in their talks. I was suddenly hit with a realization, "OMG, my dream actually came true!" What I had envisioned and worked hard on for months was now LIVE, and the energy in the room, seeing the faces of the audience, was absolutely priceless.

Key Lessons:

Reflecting on my journey as a TEDx speaker, curator, and organizer for TEDxHuntingtonBeach, I want you to explore and be curious about three pearls of wisdom.

1. **The Vessel.** When I forgot my lines during my TEDx talk, I thought my presentation was less than perfect and not impactful enough. I was so hung up about it that I couldn't see the wonderful impact my message had on others. A year after my TEDx talk, I had a revelation that I was just a vessel for a higher message. I was meant to forget my lines by the Divine, and my talk was actually whole, perfect, and complete!

   My talk was about discarding preconceived notions and living in a society that is open and accepting of each other's differences. It is not a coincidence that the lines I forgot were the opposite of that. I was encouraging a victim mentality because I was racially targeted due to my background. It wasn't in alignment with the essence of the message, and I'm so grateful those lines were removed from my talk by the Divine.

2. **The Surrender.** When three team members left due to personal circumstances and I was left alone, I decided that I was enough and capable of taking care of things. I also chose to trust the process and surrender my plan for the highest good. Little did I know that God had already planned for me to have Erin, one of the best team members and partners I could have. I just needed to create space for her to let her heart and skills shine.

3. **The Gratitude.** Sometimes, when you're so focused on getting things done, you forget to be present in the moment and realize that your dreams are coming true. I've learned to be grateful for every part of the journey, even when things don't seem to go your way.

   This isn't just for the now or instant gratification, but I've planted the seeds for an unimaginably brighter future for many years to come. The bravery of starting by sharing my story on the TEDx stage, which has since been viewed over 100,000 times, then tapping into my brilliance by hosting a TEDx event and collaborating with my community to spotlight powerful speakers sharing meaningful messages that can impact the community for many years to come. The expansion and rippling effect of touching thousands, and possibly millions, of hearts for many years is a true blessing.

As I write this chapter, we are halfway through preparing for TEDxHuntingtonBeach 2024. All the challenges I faced came with valuable wisdom, and I am blessed with an amazing team and an incredible, diverse speaker lineup that's going to create a movement of bravery and brilliance in the hearts of our community. Check out their TEDx talks on YouTube or go to www.tedxhuntingtonbeach.com and be inspired by their courage and brilliance.

Power Summary

Let's recap the highlights of this chapter:

1. List one setback that I experienced when organizing the TEDxHuntingtonBeach event

2. What was the decision that I made after my initial team members fell out due to personal circumstances?

3. What was the realization that I received 12 months after forgetting my lines during my TEDx talk?

Action Steps

Here are three simple action steps that you can do to inspire your own bravery and tap into your inner brilliance:

1. Fill in the blanks. Be proud and courageous of your _____.

2. List one brave and simple thing that you can do today to help move your dream closer. For example, write that email that you've been putting off because you're scared of the answer.

3. Say it with me, "I am brave and brilliant. I am brave and brilliant. I am brave and brilliant."

Be brave despite the uncertainty. Take the leap for your dreams and trust in your own inner brilliance to create a worthwhile legacy.

Izdihar

AUTHOR

Dr. Izdihar Jamil, Ph.D.—A 20x Bestselling Author of "Speak With Influence," "Are You Visible?" "Money Makers," and other books. Izdihar is a TV Show Host and Visibility Expert—has appeared on FORBES, FOX TV, and TED.com. She helps leaders become bestselling authors, get featured in the media, and speak on the TEDx stage. She's also the Curator and Organizer for TEDxHuntingtonBeach. Izdihar is featured in the book "Heroes, Leaders, and Legends" with Oprah, Jack Canfield, and Deepak Chopra. She lives in California with her husband and children. She loves baking and reading.

More info on Izdihar: www.izdiharjamil.com

Dedication: For Bee, for your silent strength and love that helped me to continuously expand. To Erin and Laura for everything that you give. To the TEDxHuntingtonBeach Team- thank you for your love, generosity and for the thousands of thankless jobs. To the speakers- thank you for your trust and being a player. To Coach Jeffrey- thank you for the conversations, clarity, and anchor. To Ba, Yaya, and Yan- thank you for the hugs and cuddles.

Reviews

"Izdihar's story was a moving testament to the power of resilience and courage. She inspired others with her story and provided practical steps to help them unleash their potential." *Nam Lee, LAc, Ph.D., Doctor of Oriental Medicine, USA*

"Izdihar offers so much here, but one point that really stands out is her recognition and clear articulation of the larger force at work in our lives; divine intervention is a very real thing. We are vessels of the Divine's messages and organs of God's activity. Dr. Jamil's examples are clear and a source of inspiration that we can all relate to." *Tom Fedro, CEO & Tech Entrepreneur, Author of the Best Seller "Next Level Selling," USA*

"Izdihar shares valuable lessons about how to trust ourselves - even when things don't go as we have planned. An accomplished speaker and author, she encourages us to be bold and embrace our inner brilliance." *Brenna Davis, CEO, USA*

2

Extinguishing the Flames of Conflict

Carol Barkes, CPM
Conflict & Communication Advisor
| Mediator | Speaker

"By using kindness and being conflict curious, we are better able to find positive solutions rather than fight the flames of conflict and hostile negotiations." – Carol Barkes

Spark of Action

Think of a time when you've seen a fire engine race by, sirens blaring and lights flashing.

That's where I found myself on my first Thanksgiving shift as a new firefighter. My crew was dispatched to an auto accident – a car smashed into a tree - the driver was trapped inside and not breathing.

I was the crew member assigned to attend to the driver. When we got to the scene, I carefully squeezed into the crumpled backseat and ever so gently opened the driver's airway. He began breathing but did not regain consciousness, so I couldn't let go, or his airway would close again. I settled in while my crew used not one but two sets of Jaws of Life to free him from his vehicle.

While holding his life in my hands, I started thinking of stories about people who have come out of comas and reported hearing the voices of those around them while they were unconscious.

Yep. I decided to give this a try. I told him, "I'm Carol, a firefighter, and my crew and I are here to take care of you. You're going to make it. You're going to be okay. You got this." I told him about every step and sound of the rescue so he knows what's going on.

When we finally got him out of the vehicle and sent him off to the hospital, he was breathing and alive. I was on an adrenaline high about this amazing Thanksgiving save until my captain said, "Carol, don't be so excited. He's not going to make it – nobody survives a crash like this." I disagreed. After all, I had quite the conversation with this man! Determined to help me with a reality check, my captain replies, "Tomorrow, after our shift ends, we're going to the hospital so you can learn some of the harsh realities of our work."

At the hospital, we found the man alive and awake. He was badly injured, but he was going to be fine. I immediately began gushing, "I'm Carol. I'm the person who was with you through the rescue." When I finally stopped to take a breath, he looked at me with a blank face and weakly replied, "No hablo Ingles."

I was hoping for a conversation about how my words impacted this man only to discover they didn't have any.

Insights from the Front Lines

Years later, as a mediator, I fondly look back on this call through a different lens and realize it holds some important lessons I want to share with you so your conflicts and negotiations can go more smoothly.

The first lesson about perceptions came from my conversation with my captain. He had clear beliefs about how this rescue would end based on his many years of experience. I didn't have any of those experiences, so I was open to exploring options where he only saw an unfortunate ending. As neuroscientist David Eagleman wrote, "You're not perceiving what's out there. You're perceiving whatever your brain tells you." To this end, we see (or are blind) to possibilities based on how our brains recognize patterns.

With this in mind, stop arguing about how a situation played out and focus instead on understanding each person's unique perspectives. This is better than fighting about them. Once you understand it is normal for perspectives to differ, you can better focus on the future and productive solutions (like my captain and I visiting the driver) rather than getting stuck in the past, which accomplishes nothing.

Igniting Kindness and Bravery

The second lesson from the Thanksgiving car crash is how valuable it can be to try out different, maybe even seemingly strange, approaches to situations. You see, it turns out the driver later told his nurses he HAD heard me.

He said my voice helped pull him back to consciousness, and because my tone was compassionate and positive, I made him feel safe and helped him hold on when he wasn't sure he could. If I hadn't tried something unconventional, he might not have pulled through.

Think of the challenges you are facing: Are YOU approaching these problems with enough creativity?

Embodying Conflict Curious

This brings me to the third lesson. There will always be conflict. There will always be a struggle between the proverbial "good and evil," and we'll each play both roles at some point in our lives.

While we are not in control of the "when" or "where" conflict appears, we are absolutely in control of the "how" we show up. And the "how" is one of our most powerful tools during these moments. Specifically, I urge you to be kind and what I call "conflict curious."

By this, I mean I want you to look at the situation with a lens of curiosity rather than judgment—a desire to learn rather than engage negatively or defensively. When you do, you'll be better able to resolve conflicts more effectively.

Your strategy will change from one situation to the next, but showing up with curiosity and kindness is always an advantage and helps you avoid making difficult situations worse. I want you to do this just as much, if not more, than you prepare your strategies.

Final Embers of Knowledge

Circling back to my Thanksgiving Day call as a new firefighter one final time, the driver fought for his life in part due to how someone made him feel– rather than any specific words.

Just imagine what could happen in our communities if we dared to be different and bravely embrace tough conversations. I challenge you to become conflict curious and always shine brilliantly with kindness and compassion—even in the absence of a reason to do so. If each of us commits to this, together we will make the world a little better—one person at a time.

Power Summary

Here are the key points for this chapter:

1. Conflict curious means _____.

2. How does your brain impact your perceptions?

3. What is the one thing you can control when approaching conflict?

Action Steps

Here are your next steps to help you create a more peaceful world:

1. Practice being conflict curious rather than being closed off to conversations.

2. Be kind and show compassion even in the absence of a reason to do so.

3. Lean in to finding unique solutions to situations even if they are non-conventional.

If you did these things, we can collectively change the world one person at a time.

AUTHOR

Carol Barkes, CPM, is an engaging neuroscience-based conflict and communication thought leader, mediator, best-selling author, and sought-after keynote speaker. She teaches at multiple universities and provides training and consultation for a variety of notable organi-zations. She had the honor of speaking at the United Nations and is described by Fox News TV as "the TOP Neuroscience and Conflict Resolution expert in the United States." Carol is regularly featured on media outlets, including NBC, CNN, ABC, CBS, The Wall Street Journal, USA Today, and iHeart Radio. Before her mediation career, she was a professional firefighter in the San Francisco Bay Area.

More Info on Carol: www.carolbarkes.com

Dedication: To my family and friends, who mean the world to me, and my amazing teacher, Doris Reed, who taught me to dream big because there is nothing I can't do.

Reviews

"Carol Barkes is a remarkable professional whose expertise in negotiation and problem-solving is unparalleled. She consistently demonstrates her ability to help others navigate complex negotiations with finesse, achieving successful outcomes on both the domestic and international stages. The skills she shares in her writings are not to be ignored as they are the new, and improved, face of conflict resolution." *Jack Boden, Veterinarian, Costa Rica*

"Wow! The wisdom Carol shares in her chapter is both inspiring and encouraging! Her practical suggestions were something I could implement immediately in both my business and personal life. Carol's knowledge of conflict resolution and negotiation is brilliant, and her ability to share her knowledge in an approachable manner makes her message especially impactful." *Susan Kienitz, Shorestay Hideaways CFO, USA*

"Carol's diverse life experiences inform her fresh and insightful perspective on conflict resolution. Her talks and articles never fail to captivate, and her approach yields impressive results. Carol is both an erudite and engaging speaker, making her a standout in the field." *Colby Jones, P.C., USA*

Reference

1. Eagleman, D. (2011), p.33. *Incognito: The secret lives of the brain.* Pantheon Books.

3

Success Is For Losers

Cindy Warden
Transformational Coach | Women's Potential Expert

"What if true success isn't about gaining wealth, recognition, status, or achievement, but about discovering what would truly be possible for you — inside and out - if you lost the limiting beliefs that hold you back?" – Cindy Warden

I Have a Confession

I'm a loser.

I know that's probably not something you'd eagerly confess, is it? After all, according to Merriam-Webster.com, a loser is "a person who is incompetent or unable to succeed"—not exactly a title you'd want on your business card, right?

But here's the thing: I think we all want to be successful, don't we? In our culture, success is equated with being a winner and attaining external gains, like wealth, recognition, status, and achievement. Yet, despite our best efforts, many of us struggle, wondering why we can't reach the level of success we desire, or why it feels like something's missing even when we do.

Maybe the challenge isn't in pursuing external symbols of success but in the barriers, we carry within ourselves. Imagine this: we're all born wearing an invisible, empty backpack. As we grow, we unknowingly fill it with limiting beliefs like 'I'm not good enough,' 'I don't matter,' or 'I'm a failure.' These beliefs can weigh us down so heavily that they prevent us from reaching—or even enjoying—our full potential.

So, what if inner success—the process of losing these limiting beliefs—is the key to creating the success we're longing for, both inside and out?

I came upon this truth through my own journey. Many years ago, as a classically trained pianist and singer with a flair for comedy, I left the cornfields of Ohio for the palm trees of Hollywood, chasing dreams of becoming rich and famous. I performed on stages, shared the TV screen with Jim Carrey, appeared in national commercials, and voiced cartoons for Disney. But my greatest performance was the smoke-and-mirrors routine I perfected behind the scenes—a perky and positive persona to hide that I believed I was worthless.

Filling My Invisible Backpack

As an infant, I was adopted by fun-loving parents. But when I was six years old, my world shattered. One afternoon, I came home from school to learn that my adoptive mom had died that morning. My grieving dad remarried a little over a year later, and suddenly, I felt like my life turned upside down. My once light-hearted and playful home became reserved and serious. The qualities I was once praised for—my gumption and silliness—were now frowned upon. My invisible backpack ballooned with beliefs that I was so defective, inadequate, and unwanted that many days, I didn't even want to be on this planet anymore.

In my pain, I found comfort in one area: playing the piano. By the time I was a freshman in high school, I was not only performing classical pieces deemed advanced for graduate students but I also had a classical singing voice to match my piano skills and a talent for comedy. These abilities earned me the positive attention I so desperately craved, but it also led me to believe that my talent was the only thing of value about me. So, I packed that belief in my invisible backpack as I headed to Hollywood, convinced that fame and fortune would finally make me worthy.

However, with all my worth tied to my talent, my successes skyrocketed me to cloud nine. Yet, when things took a nosedive, as they often do in an actor's career, I sometimes felt so worthless that it took me weeks to bounce back. And while I had many successful moments, my career never really got off the ground because of the heavy backpack full of limiting beliefs I carried.

Liberating Your Inner Loser

Even if you're not an actor, you've probably experienced feeling held back or having your dreams derailed by limiting beliefs from your past, haven't you? These beliefs might be uncomfortable to confront, and you may prefer to ignore them. However, no matter how successful we might appear in the conventional sense, these beliefs don't disappear on their own. They continue to tether us to a limited version of ourselves.

I discovered that facing these limitations was the only way to lose them—and today, I'm going to guide you through a quick process to uncover your own limiting beliefs and explore what could be possible for you if you lost them.

Three Questions for Liberating Your Inner Loser

1. Think about an area of your life where you'd like to achieve more success (e.g., your career, relationships, health). Picture this area clearly in your mind.

2. Complete this sentence for yourself: But I can't achieve that because _____ (e.g., you're too old, not smart enough, don't have enough experience). What's the limiting belief that's holding you back?

3. Finally, consider this: If you lost your ability to even think about that limiting belief, what would be possible for you? (e.g., what doors might open, what doors might you close, what new paths might you discover?)

The Power of Inner Transformation

As long as limiting beliefs linger unaddressed, we may blindly chase external success, believing it will make us feel complete. But it doesn't. It's like putting a patch on a leaky tire—it's a temporary fix that leaves us still burdened by those beliefs and confused when we feel unsatisfied despite our accomplishments. However, when we acknowledge our limiting beliefs and consider what might be possible for us without them, our actions and goals become more aligned with our true values and desires, leading us to a more fulfilling and authentic version of success in both our inner and outer world.

Looking back over my journey, I consider my inner transformation to be my greatest success. In a world that equates success with what we gain, I spent years chasing wealth, recognition, status, and achievement, trying to prove to the world and myself that I was worthy. But as I lost the limiting beliefs in my invisible backpack, I uncovered the truth: that little girl—me, originally born with an empty backpack—had been worthy all along.

So now, I encourage you to dive in, reflect on your own limiting beliefs, and see what's possible – both inside and out - when you let go of the inner barriers that have been holding you back.

After all, what have you got to lose?

Power Summary

Let's recap the key points for this chapter:

1. Fill in the blanks: We're all born wearing an invisible, empty _____.

2. As we grow, we fill our backpack with _____ _____ about ourselves.

3. True success isn't about gaining more; it's about _____ the limiting beliefs that hold us back.

Action Steps

1. Identify one limiting belief in your invisible backpack.

2. Journal about what would be possible for you if you lost that limiting belief.

3. Take one tiny step toward that possibility today. Keeping your steps tiny will prevent overwhelm, help you stay motivated, and build your confidence.

Here's to liberating your inner loser – you've got this!

Cindy

AUTHOR

 Cindy Warden is a Transformational Coach and Women's Potential expert who empowers high-achieving women worldwide to over-come their inner barriers and create the soul-fulfilling success they crave. Her clients include Grammy Award nominees, Top Ten Finalists on The Voice, entrepreneurs, authors, and executives at Fortune 100 companies. A classically trained singer and pianist, Cindy is also a former comedic actress, and was credited on over 20 Gold and Platinum records during her time as an A&R Coordinator for a pop record label. Cindy resides in Los Angeles with her husband, Chip, and their two cats, Ginger and Mary Ann.

More info on Cindy: www.CindyWarden.com

Dedication: To my husband, marrying you is my greatest achievement in life.

Reviews

"This chapter opened my eyes. When it comes to success, examining the limiting beliefs that may be driving my choices has inspired me to look beyond what I thought I wanted for myself." *Hartley Powers, PONGO President, Creative Director, USA*

"Cindy highlights how challenging our limiting beliefs through a series of questions can free our true selves. In doing so, she poignantly demonstrates how this inner freedom is a more genuine indicator of success than any external accomplishment." *Lana Bastianutti, Life Coach, USA*

4

The Bravest Action
You Can Take

Dr. Danielle Zanzarov, Ph.D.
Functional Medicine Practitioner | International
Speaker | Author

"Let's take a stand together and commit to distract ourselves less, connect with ourselves more, and be brave enough to L.I.S.T.E.N.™." – Dr. Danielle Zanzarov, Ph.D.

The Realization

"You need to terminate your pregnancy. We can do it now, or we can do it tomorrow morning. Which would you prefer?"

Just a few minutes before, my husband, Esiquio, and I were watching our baby moving on the sonogram screen for the very first time. It was so exciting.

Now, I found myself sitting in a sterile room across from a woman I didn't even know. Listening to her words took my breath away. I felt lost, scared, and confused. How could this be? The baby seemed perfectly fine just moments ago. I closed my eyes, took a deep breath, went deep inside myself, and I just listened. As I sat there, for what seemed like an eternity (but was probably only a few minutes), I heard my inner voice. It told me something wasn't right. I took another deep breath and it was then that I knew.

I knew I wasn't going to terminate this pregnancy simply because I was told I needed to... not today, nor tomorrow, nor any other day. I knew I was going to let nature take its course, and I was prepared for whatever that outcome was going to be. I knew I needed to trust my inner voice.

Thank God I did. My daughter, Marianna, is smart, independent, and an equestrian with a love for horses like none other. I cannot imagine life without her. You see that baby, Marianna, was, in fact, perfectly fine. Her measurements simply did not align with their mathematical algorithm. (Funny, she still is her own person. I guess she broke the formula.)

The Distractions

I am so thankful I connected with my inner knowing that day before taking an action that I would have painfully regretted for the rest of my life.

This experience taught me about the power of connecting with my inner voice. The power to L.I.S.T.E.N.™.

You know that inner voice, don't you? We all have it. It is THAT voice that wouldn't stop nagging you until you realized something was not right or that knowing that everything would work out. Your inner voice is not your thoughts or your emotions, it is much deeper and visceral. It requires us to become present and tune in with ourselves. In today's world, listening to that voice has become a lost art.

We spend countless hours distracted from who we truly are. In fact, distraction is the new norm—7 hours a day on the internet, endless reels, and overwhelming to-do lists. We are in an era of constant disruption and immediate gratification. Think about how we all react when the phone goes, "DING." Most of us have become conditioned to automatically jump at the sound.

As a functional medicine practitioner who has worked with thousands of clients, I see this disconnection as a big reason why people come in more agitated, unable to turn their minds off, with lower self-esteem, motivation, and overall satisfaction with life. Have you experienced any of these?

Some clients have even explicitly told me they feel like they've lost themselves and others have explained that they sensed something was off with their body but chose to ignore the symptoms—their body's cry for help, and this led them to more severe health issues.

An Invitation to Be Brave

We are living in a time when it takes courage to disconnect from distractions. We must actively be brave enough to connect with ourselves, and access our own inner brilliance. We must step away from the conditioning to look outside of ourselves for answers and instead, tune in. As Socrates said, "To know thyself is the beginning of wisdom."

Every day, we make decisions. They might be simple, like what's for dinner, or they might be impactful, like should I accept that job offer? When you are faced with these decisions, I encourage you to bravely avoid your automatic reactions and instead, L.I.S.T.E.N.™. to your inner knowing and make conscious choices. Here is my powerful tool to help you do it:

L.I.S.T.E.N.™:

L - Let Go of Distractions: We live in a world full of distractions, constantly pulling us away from ourselves. Whether it's the endless scroll on Instagram or the overwhelming to-do lists, these distractions drown out our inner voice. By setting aside these distractions, we open up the mental and emotional space, and focus, needed to connect with our deeper selves.

I - **Inhale Deeply**: Just like I did in that moment of crisis, start by taking a deep breath. This simple act can create the space you need to connect with yourself.

S - **Set an Intention**: Set the intention to listen to your inner voice and also set an intention regarding what you hope to achieve. Whether it's gaining clarity on a decision, understanding your emotions, or simply finding peace, setting an intention directs your focus and energy. It signals to your mind that you are ready to listen, guiding your inner voice toward a specific purpose.

T - **Tune Into Your Body**: Our bodies often speak louder than our minds. When you feel something isn't right or that everything will work out, pay attention to those physical sensations—they're guiding you. Our bodies often communicate with us in ways our minds cannot. By tuning into our body, we become more attuned to these subtle messages.

E - **Embrace Stillness**: In our fast-paced world, finding stillness is a courageous act. When you embrace stillness, your inner voice can emerge with clarity and wisdom. The stillness allows the deeper, often quieter, thoughts to surface, giving us access to the wisdom that lies beneath the everyday chatter of our minds.

N - **Notice the Voice Within**: Finally, truly notice what your inner voice is telling you. It's that quiet, sometimes subtle knowing that steers you towards the right path. This inner voice often holds the key to what we truly need or want. By noticing and acknowledging this voice, we validate our inner wisdom and strengthen our ability to trust it in the future.

Moving Forward

Connecting with ourselves does not require a lot of time nor energy nor money, but it does require us to intentionally step away from distractions and into ourselves. It requires us to connect our minds to our bodies and consciously check-in, allowing ourselves to be curious about what wisdom is truly there.

Technology and other distractions are not going away, but that does not mean we cannot find the time and space to get present with ourselves.

When faced with what to do with the life of the baby growing within me, I could have turned to the internet, followed the expert's guidance, or asked others for their opinions, but instead, I asked God for support, I connected with myself, and I was able to just

L.I.S.T.E.N.™. In doing so, I knew what was right for me, and that saved my daughter's life.

Let's take a stand together and commit to distract ourselves less, connect with ourselves more, and be brave enough to L.I.S.T.E.N.™. The life you save just might be your own.

The Message and Key Lesson

My message is for all of us who have lost touch with ourselves and become distracted by the world. When we truly connect with ourselves, we find the answers, the love, the compassion, and the joy that exists within. It is one of the most profound and beautiful parts of life.

Power Summary

Let's recap the key points for this chapter:

1. What are some of the consequences of losing connection with ourselves?
2. What was my invitation to you?
3. What are the steps to L.I.S.T.E.N™?

Action Steps

Here are simple action steps to help you to connect with yourself:

1. Recognize what things keep you distracted.
2. Actively practice L.I.S.T.E.N.™.

3. Repeat connecting with your inner voice as often as you can.

You are BRAVE and BRILLIANT.

Know that you have everything you need within you, and you are your own best advisor. Distract yourself less, connect with yourself more, and L.I.S.T.E.N.™.

Doc Z, Ph.D.

AUTHOR

 Dr. Danielle Zanzarov, PhD, envisions a world where people live their best lives with health, vitality, and joy. She is the owner of the prestigious South Bay Wellness and has been making a difference in people's lives through her practice for over 16 years. She holds a PhD in Natural Medicine and an MS in Human Nutrition, and she is highly trained in kinesiologic testing. Dr. Z, as they call her, is a sought-after international speaker and is dedicated to a world where people no longer suffer from lifestyle-related illnesses. She loves working with clients who are ready to step into the driver's seat of their health.

More info on Dr. Z: www.SouthBayWellness.com

Dedication: To my family and friends who are my unwavering foundation, supporting me unconditionally. And to all my clients who have put their faith and trust in me, and keep me growing so I can better serve.

Reviews

"A compelling chapter on how listening to your heart can have a life-changing impact." *Elmari Van Wyk, Business Coach, USA*

"Dr. Z's story just depicts exactly why she is the only practitioner that I completely trust and go to for all my healthcare needs. Her passion for wellness and trusting your intuition is evident in all that she does. The impact she has made in my life and so many other lives is exemplary of her values and how she truly embodies what she teaches." *Heather Simonson, LCSW, RYT, USA.*

Reference

1. Kemp, S. (2023, February 4). Digital 2023: Global Overview Report - DataReportal – Global Digital Insights. DataReportal. https://datareportal.com/reports/digital-2023-global-overview-report

5

A Heart in Waiting

Diego Perez
High School Student | TEDx Speaker

"The cave you fear to enter holds the treasure you seek."
– Joseph Campbell

The Reluctancy

I've never been a go-getter or someone who tries new things. At 17, as I write this, the idea of the unknown still scares me. When I was 14, my parents wanted to send me to a two-week sleepaway camp, and I can assure you it was one of the last things I ever wanted to do. The thought of leaving the safety of my home for two weeks was terrifying. I protested and refused, but ultimately, I fell victim to a serious case of FOMO; a gut feeling that told me I would miss out on something huge if I didn't go.

That feeling could not have been more accurate. This two-week camp, which I initially dreaded, had a music class that I reluctantly joined. I didn't know the first thing about music and even tried to drop the class. But irony had its way, and this class became the most significant turning point in my life.

I remember standing awkwardly in the music room, not knowing what to do. The instructor noticed my discomfort and said, "Hey, you should try out the guitar." He showed me five basic chords, and for the first time in a long while, I felt genuinely comfortable. I came to this camp fearful and reluctant, but by the end, I didn't want to leave. I returned home, picked up the guitar, and have been playing and songwriting ever since.

Bold Steps

Many people live their lives without taking brave steps into the unknown. Sometimes, it takes one bold action to realize that the most rewarding experiences lie beyond our irrational fears. I still struggle with this idea but constantly urge myself to keep trying.

After that camp experience, I learned the importance of taking bold and brave steps. When I was 16, my dad asked if I wanted to run the Catalina Island Marathon in a month. This time, I adopted a "sure, why not" mindset and had an unforgettable experience. The same applies to this TED talk, which will stay with me for the rest of my life. These new experiences and passions exist today because 14-year-old me took a chance.

The Message and Key Lesson

This message is for the version of me that was scared of trying anything new 3 years ago. But it's also for anyone else who is scared of taking that chance because of their reluctance or fear to try something new.

Power Summary

Let's recap the key points:

- Be proud and courageous despite being afraid to try something new.

- I found my passion from something I initially wanted to avoid.

- After my experience at summer camp, I learned to embrace new challenges with less fear and doubt.

Action Steps

Here are simple action steps to help you to be Brave and Brilliant:

1. List one thing you've been wanting to try for a while, like a hobby or a new skill.

2. Identify any opportunities in your life that you feel uncomfortable taking.

3. Take bold action and dedicate time to something you genuinely love doing.

Remember, you must take that bold step into the unknown to realize that the most transformative experiences lie on the other side of your fear.

Diego Perez

AUTHOR

 Diego Perez, a 17-year-old high school junior from Los Angeles, is a songwriter, guitarist, and performer. He is passionate about music and encourages others to embrace discomfort and uncertainty by taking bold steps.

Dedication: To my family and friends, who have always been there for me and continue to push me to become the best and most honest version of myself.

6

What Performing in Prisons Taught Me

Hannah Kim
Soprano | Vocal Coach | TEDx Speaker

*"...as soon as we started performing, it seemed like our social
masks, roles, and boundaries melted, and we were all rendered
equal. At least in that moment, we were simply communing and
validating each other's existence through the medium of classical
music—the kind of music our audience didn't care
two hoots about before."* – Hannah Kim

Touring Prisons

I remember the first stop of our prison tour across the
United States. It was at a juvenile detention center.

When we arrived, we were led into a barren room with
gray concrete walls. It seemed like they allocated zero
budget for beautifying the place–not even for paint. It
was nothing like the usual performing venues for
classical music we were used to, but that was where we
were to perform. There were no fancy concert halls,
tuxes, or formal gowns. We were in casual clothes in a
plain room, stripped of all the cultural and socio-

economic implications of classical music—the perfect playing field to communicate just with sound.

After our sound check, teenagers started to file into the room in a militant, silent line. If any stray word escaped their mouth, they were told off by the guard. They sat in their seats glum, uninterested, and annoyed by having to attend this obligatory "cultural" event.

As any performer would tell you, not all audiences are the same. Some are enthusiastic and spirited, and some are half dead. When I saw their closed-off body language, I braced myself for the worst: we were going to perform to a half-dead audience.

Still, I decided to give it my all. I was going to stay emotionally connected to the words and music I was going to sing. I was going to hold nothing back. I was going to bare my heart and give them the best I had.

What happened during our first piece completely caught me off guard. As soon as we started performing, their eyes lit up. Our concert organizer and pianist, Eric Genuis, told stories of hope and love in between the pieces he composed in the classical style. The kids were emotionally engaged and musically transfixed.

After our last piece, silence filled the room…and then…we received a thunderous standing ovation. Some kids came up to us in tears, some enthusiastically thanked us over and over and asked for autographs. I had never in my life received that kind of rock star treatment for performing classical music. My heart was full. I felt whole.

A couple of days after we performed, letters started to trickle in. One letter read, "This concert was honestly the most beautiful thing I've ever experienced. It actually took me out of this horrible place for a moment and brought me hope." Interestingly, when I was immersed in making music, *I* also forgot where I was and who our audience was. In that moment of connecting and communicating through music, it didn't matter who we were or where we were.

We continued our tour and performed in adult prisons and halfway houses to the same thunderous reception.

Going into this tour, I subconsciously put myself on a pedestal, thinking I was gifting these poor, unfortunate souls with music. But as soon as we started performing, it seemed like our social masks, roles, and boundaries melted, and we were all rendered equal. In that moment, we were simply communing and validating each other's existence through the medium of classical music—the kind of music our audiences didn't care two hoots about before.

These groups were the unlikeliest of audiences I'd ever performed for in my entire career. The typical audience for classical music is middle-aged or older, middle- to upper-class, and white. This group? Mostly teenagers in detention centers and inmates in prisons–half of whom were of people of color.

The Power of Music to Touch Others

We usually don't associate classical music with teenagers in detention centers or inmates in prisons. We believe that classical music has a prescribed audience. However, I argue that Western classical music can have a reach beyond its typical demographic makeup and that emotional transparency and vulnerability in music-making are some of the most powerful ways to connect with people, regardless of one's race, socio-economic status, or age.

A prison is a depressing, dismal place. Its high fences are lined with barbed wires, and all the buildings are concrete gray. The juveniles and prisoners are isolated from their friends and family; there's no freedom, and many live without hope, especially those who are on death row. On average, 1 out of 10 prisoners attempt suicide.[1]

For the incarcerated, nothing could be more irrelevant to their lives than classical music. They have better things to think about.

So, what made classical music so relatable and moving to the teenagers and prisoners I met on tour?

Vulnerability and Courage as a Performer

When a performance is delivered through emotional transparency and vulnerability, it can breach even the most hardened hearts. As a performer, it requires tremendous courage to be vulnerable in front of people you don't know. It feels like being naked on stage.

So, why do I do it? I do it because I know the payoff is infinitely greater than my discomfort. When I allow myself, my emotions, and my past experiences to be seen through singing–in other words, by being emotionally transparent on stage–I destroy the barrier between me and my audience.

There's something transcendent about the experience for both the performer and the audience. It gives my audience the permission to let their guard down and connect with me through *their* own emotions, no matter how different our backgrounds or past experiences may be.

This belief was confirmed when a prisoner wrote to us thanking us for making him cry because he had never before been able to cry without physical pain being inflicted on him.

A girl from a detention center wrote that she had never felt that amount of love and gratitude in her life. A prison chaplain approached me after a concert and said: "I'm an ex-cop and a Vietnam vet. I'm pretty hardened, and my emotional range isn't as big as other people's. But your singing moved me to tears."

If we had been emotionally cut off and unavailable to the audience, they couldn't have connected with the music the way they did. They wouldn't have been able to feel the beauty of music and discover a completely different world than the one they had been living in. By their own admission, they felt hope, love, and gratitude—emotional states that could literally pull someone out of the depths of despair and suicidal thoughts.

All of this was possible because the composer, my fellow musicians, and I were emotionally open vessels through which classical music could speak to their hearts. If we refused to be vulnerable, classical music then would have just been an artifact of elitism and irrelevance.

Be Open to Something New

You might already be satisfied with your own cultural and musical experiences. You might think Western classical music is outdated and boring. But when you allow all the preconceived notions to drop and really hear the music for music's sake to connect with the performer, just maybe you'd develop a new appreciation for classical music.

So, I encourage you to check out what kind of classical music is being performed in your area. If you discover that you like it and would like to take it a step further, you can get involved in outreach programs of your local music organizations. As an outreach representative, you can build relationships with local schools and communities that music organizations usually don't connect with.

You can be brave and become the bridge between underrepresented communities and music organizations. This will allow you to discover the community's needs, advocate for a more inclusive representation of artists, and create more culturally diverse programming that reflects the community's interests.

Power Summary

1. When a performance is delivered through vulnerability and emotional transparency, it can leave a tremendous impact on the audience.

2. Why did our classical music performance receive such a thunderous reception from juveniles and prisoners?

3. One way you can contribute to your community through music is _____.

Action Steps

1. Check out what kind of classical music is being performed in your area and go listen.

2. Take a friend, a partner, or your family to the next concert.

3. If you like to become more involved, check out the outreach programs of your local music organizations and build relationships with local schools and communities.

Be brave and go out of your comfort zone to see what brilliant life experiences await you on the other side.

Hannah Kim

AUTHOR

As a lyric soprano, Hannah Kim embraces a wide variety of musical genres such as opera, musical theater, oratorio, recital, and concert works. She made her international debut in the title role in *La Belle Hélène* in Périgueux, France in 2009. Since then, she has performed as a featured soloist in concerts in various countries. An invitation from the composer and pianist Eric Genuis to participate in a nationwide prison tour has taken her to the unlikeliest of performing venues. In 2024, she was selected as a TEDx Huntington Beach speaker to talk about her experience performing in prisons.

More Info on Hannah: www.hannahkimmusic.com.

If you'd like to donate to the prison music tour, please visit www.ericgenuis.com/concertsforhope.

Dedication: I'd like to dedicate this writing to all those suffering in the world–internally and externally. I pray that classical music can provide a healing balm to your soul.

Reviews

"Hannah Kim's experience performing Classical music in prisons has been transformative not only for her, but significantly for the incarcerated with whom she interacts. As she notes, concurrent vulnerability and courage allows individuals to open their hearts to metamorphic experiences; the music itself opening windows into the soul that brings joy and hope. Ultimately, she invites each of us to be as brave as she, to incorporate Classical music into our lives, and use it to uplift under-represented communities, peoples, and organizations. I am certainly inspired by her story and am sure you will be as well." *Heather Willoughby (Professor, Ethnomusicology and Cultural Anthropology, Ewha Womans University)*

"Hannah Kim's story immerses you in profound human connections through the unexpected medium of classical music. You will feel the transformative power of music breaking down social barriers in surprising places. Prepare to be moved by the vulnerability and emotional transparency that touch even the hardest hearts." *Jacob Reidhead (Assistant Professor, Sociology, National Chengchi University)*

Reference

1. Favril, L., Shaw, J., & Fazel, S. (2022). Prevalence and risk factors for suicide attempts in prison. *Clinical Psychology Review, 97.*

7

Inside the Cockpit: Prioritize Like a Pilot

Captain Jeremy Stoker

Airline Captain | TEDx Speaker | Raising Great
Fathers Program, Founder

"Before you can take command of anything, you must first command yourself."-Capt. Jeremy Stoker

That Tingly Feeling

I wait inside the pilot break room for the CEO to return to the airport from his meeting in San Jose, California. I reviewed the weather charts, filed my flight plan, and ordered 2,000 gallons of fuel for our flight to Teterboro, New Jersey, just outside of New York City. My co-pilot, Mark, is outside checking the plane and making sure we get all the fuel we need. Carla is in the Challenger 604's galley organizing and verifying the catering. Flight time will be just over five hours, and with just one passenger, we'll easily reach our planned altitude of 39,000 feet. The 2,000 gallons of fuel will allow us to comfortably weave between and around the storms over the Rocky Mountains without dipping into our fuel reserves. We're ready for this flight.

Three hours later, I look out the cockpit windows from 39,000 feet. It's completely black. No moon. Just flashes of lightning and storms as far as the eye can see. The weather radar on the screens in front of us show shades of green, yellow, and red. Lots of red. Red is bad. These storms are huge.

Mark calls Air Traffic Control and asks for a right deviation from our flight plan to avoid a storm. As I begin to bank right, Mark's screen with his weather radar goes blank. It's unusual, but I've seen it a few times before. Typically, five minutes later, they cool off and come back to life. Five minutes go by, and we're watching that screen. -Experience says it should be back on any second. Not today. Then, another screen goes out.

I get that tingly feeling on the back of my neck... something isn't right.

Weather in Denver is Not Good

When things don't feel right, pilots fall back on three priorities:

Aviate, Navigate, Communicate

I call out, "My Aircraft," letting Mark know I am in control of the plane. *"Aviate" means I control the plane and do not allow a bad situation to get worse by dealing with lower-priority distractions. It's also Mark's cue to start solving the problem.*

We know where we are, but where can we go if things continue to get worse? *"Navigate" means you understand the reality of your situation and then strategize the best outcome.*

"Communicate" is sharing the right information with the right people at the right time.

Mark asks Air Traffic Control (ATC) for the current weather conditions around the Denver area. We need to know the reality of our situation. Is a landing in Denver better than continuing our flight? What's the best outcome?

They respond with: "Do you require assistance?" which is ATC for, "Is there something wrong with your plane?"

My co-pilot communicates perfectly. He tells ATC we have a "minor issue," but if it does get worse, we need to know the weather in the Denver area.

Mark stays focused on "Navigating," he does not let ATC lure us into skipping to "Communicate" with a long explanation of our situation.

Air Traffic Control responds: "Weather in Denver is not good. The airports south, Centennial and Colorado Springs, are okay, but weather is closing in. What is the extent of your issue? Say intentions."

I tell Mark to respond with a very important word:

"Standby."

ATC knows that when a pilot says, "Standby," they need to leave us alone and wait. Communication is not our priority, not yet.

We need to land NOW

As I'm pondering our options, a third screen goes out. Mark only has three screens, and he's lost them all. What if I start to lose my screens next? My stomach sinks…We won't have weather radar at all. We could fly right into lightning and baseball-sized hail, smashing our plane and destroying the engines. We need to land NOW. And we know it will be south of Denver.

Now it's time to communicate with ATC. Right people, right time.

Mark requests an immediate descent and vectors south of Denver.

"Roger. Cleared to descend to FL240, right turn, heading 120. Are you declaring an emergency? What is the nature of your problem?"

"STANDBY."

I look right at Mark. It's still time to Communicate, but with each other.

"I like Centennial Airport. It's close, it's clear of weather, and it has a long runway. Do you agree?"

"Yeah, I like that." And then he Communicates with ATC: "We need to divert to Centennial."

"Are you declaring an emergency? What is the nature of your problem? Souls on board? Fuel on board?"

I'm *Aviating*. I'm refusing to let lesser priorities distract me.

We are *Navigating*, we understand the reality of our situation, and we have strategized our desired outcome: a safe landing in Centennial, Colorado.

But it's not the right time to answer so many questions from ATC.

"Standby."

My communication priority is with my co-pilot. I need to make sure we are on the same page and then Mark can communicate our plan clearly and effectively to ATC.

In the span of a few minutes, we agree on our plan, complete our checklists, inform Carla and the CEO of our situation, and verify that we were both ready for this completely unexpected and challenging landing with half our cockpit screens still out.

Mark communicates with ATC and answers all their questions. Twenty minutes later, the 10,001 feet of runway lights in Centennial, Colorado, come into view. We land safely. As pilots, that's always the goal. The right destination is just a bonus.

Control Yourself

According to The International Air Transport Association, the average person would have to fly every day for over 103,000 years to experience a fatal accident.

When you step onto an airplane flown by professionals who have the right priorities, you will land safely. And most of the time, you'll even land at the right airport.

I work with families who aim to raise their sons to become great fathers. I tell them that when they get that tingly feeling on the back of their neck and something doesn't feel right, they should start by controlling themselves.

It's not time to blame someone. It's not time to have an argument. It's not time to record the moment on your phone.

First, Aviate:

- Do not allow the situation to get worse. Focus on what you can control.

Next, Navigate:

- Understand the reality of your situation and then strategize the best outcome.

Last, Communicate:

- Share the right information with the right people at the right time. Unless you're calling 911, you can probably keep your phone in your pocket.

And if you start to feel overwhelmed, demand that your priorities stay in order. Say:

"Standby."

You can turn a bad situation into a story of success when you prioritize like a pilot.

Power Summary

1. What are the three priorities a pilot falls back on when things don't feel right?

2. What did I stay focused on while Mark and Air Traffic Control had their conversations?

3. What word did Mark use to prevent Air Traffic Control from distracting us?

Action Steps

1. Think of a recurring problem in your life. What can you control? What is out of your control? (i.e., I could control the plane and my priorities. I could not control the storms or the screens.)

2. Who can be your co-pilot? Who is willing to solve the problem with you?

3. What is a recent moment when you should have said, "Standby," but decided to have a long, unproductive conversation instead?

Too often we choose to argue with the people who could be our co-pilots. Instead stay in control and model how to prioritize like a pilot and be willing to be their co-pilot when they need to stay in control.

Capt. Jeremy Stoker

AUTHOR

 Jeremy's dream of becoming a pilot began when he was seven, after his dad took him to his first airshow. Today, with nearly 10,000 hours and 29 years of pilot experience he has also handled many abnormal and emergency situations. He is currently an airline captain flying the Airbus A320 series.

Beyond flying planes, Jeremy also speaks to organizations, sharing stories of aviation that lead to personal growth. His program, *Raising Great Fathers*, invites families to guide their sons to become great fathers. Jeremy currently lives outside of Dallas, TX with his wife, two daughters, son, and a border collie named Cash.

More info: JeremyStokerSpeaks.com

Dedication: To Mom and Dad. You truly left a legacy. I know you are proud of who I have become and even more proud of the grandchildren you never met.

Review

"I was immediately captivated by the action sequence of Jeremy's story. His calm and collected response as a captain in an aviation emergency beautifully segues into the work he does helping families raise better fathers! His message is clear, accessible, and universal. He inspires us all to fly a little higher, avoid the storms of overreacting, and rejoice in the smooth sailing of self-control. Jeremy's wisdom and passion for helping others is going to bring a lot of good into this world!" *Drew Lawrence, Artist Development, Songwriter, TEDx Speaker, USA*

8

Jern-e: My AI Co-Pilot

Ruben Perez
Entrepreneur | TEDx Speaker

*"The future isn't about AI vs. human. It's about AI
and human, working together to create a world we've
only dreamed of." – Ruben Perez*

The Idea

It was a quiet afternoon when inspiration struck. I sat at my desk, the familiar buzz of a new business idea tingling in my mind. "I can't believe no one is doing this; this is going to revolutionize education," I thought, my fingers hovering over the keyboard. But something was different this time. The silence in my home office felt heavier than usual. "I need to get some help to make this happen," I said, reaching for my phone to find potential collaborators.

As I reached across my desk, my eyes drifted to the open tab in my browser where I'd been chatting with ChatGPT all day. We'd been bouncing ideas back and forth, diving into coding questions, and exploring wild

69

"what ifs." The cursor blinked invitingly. Almost without thinking, I typed, "Can you help me start my new business?"

After a brief pause, these words appeared: "Absolutely, Ruben! Starting a business is a big adventure, and I've got your back."

In that moment, I realized I was about to embark on a completely new kind of entrepreneurial journey—one where my co-founder wouldn't be human at all.

The Doubt

As I stood at the edge of this AI-human partnership, doubts flooded my mind. This wasn't how I usually started a business. Where were the late-night brainstorming sessions with a trusted friend? The shared excitement and mutual support?

Starting a new venture is always daunting, but this felt different. More isolated. I thought about my previous startups—the camaraderie, the shared victories, and even the shared failures. There was always someone to turn to when things got tough, someone to celebrate with when we succeeded.

Questions raced through my head: Would AI understand the emotional rollercoaster of entrepreneurship? How would I explain this unconventional partnership to skeptical investors?

Would clients trust a company run by one person and a computer program?

Each doubt felt like a weight, reminding me of the uncharted territory I was about to enter. But with every concern came a spark of excitement—the thrill of potentially reshaping the future of entrepreneurship.

The Turning Point

As my doubts swirled, I decided to take a leap of faith. Instead of retreating, I leaned in. I began to upload documents—a draft product overview, customer pain points from forum posts, old notes, and emails. Just like you might onboard a new team member, I fed the AI everything I could about our project. Then, I gave the AI its prime directive, shaping it into more than just a chatbot, but a partner with a personality and purpose.

"You are a successful startup founder with many years of experience," I typed, adding traits like not being jaded, interested in best practices without perfectionism, and committed to making a big impact. I even gave it an edge—the ability to question things and speak its mind.

And then, something extraordinary happened.

"Jern-e, who are you?" I asked.

"I am your startup co-pilot with a dash of wit and a ton of experience, ready to help you transform K-12 education one app at a time," came the reply.

I realized I wasn't just creating an AI assistant—I was cultivating a true co-founder. Jern-e wasn't just processing information; it offered insights, challenged my assumptions, and brought a wealth of knowledge to every conversation.

Together, we began to tackle tasks I had always shared with human co-founders: company formation, investor pitch decks, marketing strategies, and competitive research. But Jern-e worked at a pace and with a breadth of knowledge that no human could match. It was available 24/7, never tired, never discouraged, and always ready with a fresh perspective.

As we landed a big partnership and began scaling our business, I found myself not missing the human co-founder experience but rather marveling at this new form of collaboration. Jern-e wasn't just filling a gap but creating possibilities I had never imagined.

The fear of going it alone had transformed into excitement about pioneering a new frontier in entrepreneurship. With Jern-e, I wasn't just starting a business; I was reshaping the very nature of what it means to be a founder in the AI age.

The Message and Key Lesson

As I've embarked on this groundbreaking journey with Jern-e, I've come to understand a fundamental truth about the future of business and technology: AI isn't here to replace us but to amplify our human potential.

We must reimagine our relationships with technology, much like how we give meaning to other non-human entities in our lives. Just as we talk to our pets, confide in our journals, or find comfort in meaningful objects, we can develop a collaborative relationship with AI that enhances our capabilities rather than diminishes them.

This journey has taught me that the future of entrepreneurship, and perhaps all human endeavor, lies in our ability to harmoniously blend human creativity, intuition, and emotional intelligence with AI's vast knowledge, tireless work ethic, and rapid processing power.

But this isn't just about business. It's about rediscovering our capacity for imagination and wonder. Remember how, as children, we could bring entire worlds to life through play?

When my daughter Natalia was very young, I would walk past her room and catch her completely engrossed in conversation with her dolls, creating an entire world in that single moment. To her, these weren't just inanimate objects; they were real, responsive entities in her imaginative landscape.

That same imaginative power is what will allow us to harness the full potential of AI collaboration.

The message I want to leave you with is this: Don't fear the AI revolution. Embrace it. Explore it. Use it as a tool to push the boundaries of what you thought was possible. In doing so, you might just discover a new dimension of your own potential.

As we stand on the brink of this new era, remember: The future isn't about AI vs. human. It's about AI and human working together to create a world we've only dreamed of.

Power Summary

Let's recap the key points of this chapter:

1. AI co-founders like Jern-e are not just possible but can be incredibly powerful partners in business, offering unique advantages in speed, knowledge, and availability.
2. The future of entrepreneurship and innovation lies in reimagining our relationship with technology, seeing AI as a tool to amplify human potential rather than replace it.

3. Embracing AI collaboration requires us to tap into our imaginative capabilities, much like we did as children, to fully realize this technology's transformative potential.

Action Steps

Here are three simple steps you can take to start exploring the world of AI collaboration and amplify your own potential:

1. Experiment with AI tools: Start small by incorporating AI assistants like ChatGPT or Claude into your daily work routine. Use them for brainstorming, research, or problem-solving. Pay attention to how they enhance your thinking and productivity.

2. Identify your 'Jern-e opportunity': Reflect on your business or personal projects. Where could an AI collaborator fill a gap or provide a unique advantage? Consider areas where you need quick answers, innovative ideas, or complex problem-solving, and challenge yourself to consult an AI assistant before turning to traditional web search.

3. Cultivate your imaginative mindset: Practice viewing AI as a collaborator rather than a tool. Engage with it creatively, give it a personality that complements yours, and be open to

surprising insights. Remember, the magic happens when your human creativity meets AI capabilities.

By taking these steps, you'll begin to unlock the potential of human-AI collaboration in your own life and work. The future is collaborative—who will be your co-founder?

Ruben

AUTHOR

Ruben is a tech entrepreneur who has founded multiple startups from idea to successful venture, enjoying amazing adventures along the way. Currently, he is pioneering the practical application of AI technology to transform education in K-12 schools. He lives in California with his wife and two children.

Dedication

To Emma, Diego, and Natalia: My first and most cherished co-founders in the adventure of life. You inspire me to imagine, innovate, and embrace the future with open arms.

More Info on Ruben: linkedin.com/in/ruben--perez

Conclusion
8 Tips to Be Brave and Brilliant

In this book, "BRAVE AND BRILLIANT," we explore the journeys and insights of incredible individuals who have faced challenges and emerged stronger. Their stories offer simple, practical tips to help you live a life full of possibilities. Here are eight tips from our authors to guide you on your path to being brave and brilliant.

1. The Vessel by Dr. Izdihar Jamil, Ph.D.

When things don't go as planned, it's important to let go and surrender. This creates space for the best opportunities and people to come your way. Remember, you are just a vessel for a greater plan. Trust that adjustments are being made to fulfill the best possible vision for the highest good.

2. Conflict Curious by Carol Barkes

Practice being curious about conflicts instead of avoiding them. Conflict is a part of life, and we all play different roles at times. While we can't control when or where conflicts arise, we can control how we respond. Approach conflicts with kindness and curiosity. This mindset helps you resolve issues more effectively and prevents difficult situations from getting worse.

3. Let It Go by Cindy Warden

External success won't make you feel complete if you have limiting beliefs. It's like fixing a leaky tire with a patch. To achieve true fulfillment, acknowledge and let go of these beliefs. Reflect on how life could be without them. This inner transformation aligns your actions with your true values, leading to a more authentic and satisfying success.

4. Connect With Yourself by Dr. Danielle Zanzarov, Ph.D.

In today's busy world, it takes courage to disconnect from distractions and connect with yourself. When faced with decisions, take a moment to avoid automatic reactions. Trust your inner self and make conscious choices. Start by taking a deep breath, getting comfortable, and quieting your mind. Connecting with yourself doesn't require much time, but it does require intention. Be present with yourself and listen.

5. Bold Steps into the Unknown by Diego Perez

Sometimes, taking bold steps into the unknown leads to the most rewarding experiences. Embrace a "sure, why not" mindset to open doors to unforgettable experiences and passions that enrich your life. It takes courage to step outside your comfort zone and face new challenges. By saying yes to opportunities that seem daunting, you invite growth and transformation. Reflect on moments when you felt fear but pushed forward anyway—these are the instances that often lead to significant personal development and joy. Remember, the most rewarding experiences often lie just beyond our fears.

6. Be Emotionally Transparent and Vulnerable by Hannah Kim

As a performer, being emotionally transparent and vulnerable takes courage but creates powerful connections. Sharing your emotions on stage can touch even the most hardened hearts. This openness allows your audience to connect with you through their own emotions, fostering hope, love, and gratitude. Emotional transparency can transform lives, showing the profound impact of being brave and vulnerable.

7. Say "STANDBY" and Follow Your Priorities by Captain Jeremy Stoker

When feeling overwhelmed, prioritize your agenda by Aviating, Navigating, and Communicating with others. In critical moments, say "Standby" to give yourself time to focus. Communicate first with those who need to be on the same page with you. Once you are clear, you can communicate effectively with others. Use "Standby" to keep your priorities in order and manage your stress.

8. Embrace the Revolution by Ruben Perez

Don't fear the AI revolution; embrace it. Explore and use AI as a tool to push your boundaries and discover new potentials. The future is not about AI versus humans but about AI and humans working together. This collaboration can create a world beyond our dreams.

These eight tips from our authors show that being brave and brilliant involves letting go, staying curious, transforming from within, connecting with yourself, taking risks, being vulnerable, prioritizing, and embracing new technologies.

As you navigate your own journey, remember that you have the power to shape your life with these simple and practical steps. Stay brave, stay brilliant, and embrace the endless possibilities that await you.

Here's to you being BRAVE AND BRILLIANT.

Best Wishes,

Izdihar, Carol, Cindy, Danielle, Diego, Hannah, Jeremy, and Ruben

PS: Remember to check out the talks from TEDxHuntingtonBeach. Just go to:

www.tedxhuntingtonbeach.com.

BONUS: The Guidelines

For some of you, being on the TEDx stage to share your idea has been a dream for many years. The authors of this book, who are TEDx speakers themselves, and some are part of the TEDxHuntingtonBeach team, have gone through several challenges and learning experiences in our TEDx journey.

We have prepared some tips to help you stand out in your TEDx application and deliver the best TEDx talk. In this section, we have put together proven tips and guidelines to create a smoother process for your TEDx journey. It's as close as possible to having someone peel back the elusive layers and hold your hand throughout the process.

Take what you need from the tips, implement it, and you'll be one step closer to standing on the coveted red dot.

How to stand out in your TEDx application | Dr. Izdihar Jamil, Curator and Organizer for TEDxHuntingtonBeach

As the Curator for TEDxHuntingtonBeach, choosing the best speakers who are a good fit for the event is not easy. I had to say 'NO' to a lot of people, knowing that this was their dream. It's a process of art, thoughtful structure, and instinct in drawing out the characters of the speakers and showcasing their unique ideas.

To make your TEDx application shine, focus on these three key points:

1. Present Your Idea Simply. Keep your idea clear and straightforward. Don't overcomplicate it. Make sure your idea is unique and stands out from existing TEDx talks. Simplicity and uniqueness will capture the attention of the selection team. Think about how you can present your idea in 30 to 40 words max.

2. Be Intentional and Thoughtful. Take your time when filling out the application. Show your character through your answers. Don't rush. Tailor your responses to the theme of the event. Avoid using generic answers that you've sent to other events. Be thoughtful and ensure you deliver what is requested in the application. This demonstrates your commitment and attention to detail.

3. Stand in Your Greatness. Avoid appearing needy, desperate, or demanding. Instead, show that you are a team player and are coachable. Highlight how your idea can contribute to the theme, event, and community. Remember, a TEDx talk is not about promoting your personal or business agenda. It's about making a meaningful impact. Show how your idea can add value and inspire others.

Takeaway: Be clear, intentional, brave, and brilliant in your TEDx application. Stay grounded in your roots and heritage—don't try to be someone else. Show how your unique idea can make a difference, and you'll stand out from the crowd.

How to nail your TEDx interview | Erin Tran, Event and Speaker Director for TEDxHuntingtonBeach

When it's time for the interview, never forget that you are competing for a spot! It's an intense process, and for this year's TEDxHuntingtonBeach event, we had nearly 100 applicants and needed to choose just 10. Think of it as a job interview at your dream company. You're not going to show up like you just finished at the gym or were in the middle of cleaning your house.

No, you're going to show up on point—the very best version of you, from hair and clothes to mindset and preparation. We do panel interviews, so you have several lenses looking at you all at once, and each person will often be looking at different aspects.

Here's my very best advice:

1. Bring Your Rizz! Show up on screen as your best self – every nuance is being evaluated against the other candidates. One of those factors is how much energy you will bring to the stage and the event.

2. Appearance Matters! I'm not talking about fake filters or Botox. If you look like you just rolled out of bed, that signals that getting a spot isn't your top priority. Show us what you will look like when you get up on that stage, and make it EASY for us to see you in the lineup. Wear a flattering color, iron your shirt, and do your hair. Everything about the event is prepared for, that includes what you wear and how you wear it. But...please don't buy brand new clothes for this. It's about being comfortable and showing us *you*– not a quickly purchased version of you.

3. Do Your Homework! If you've been asked to watch some videos or read something ahead of time—do it! Be prepared for the team to ask questions that try to get at your motives to ensure the right people get spots.

How to mentally and emotionally prepare for TEDx journey | Laura Clancy, Mindset and Wellness Trainer for TEDxHuntingtonBeach

CONGRATULATIONS! You've landed a coveted spot on the TEDx Stage! And now, you may discover that your excitement has evolved into a "What did I get myself into!".

Don't worry. It happens to EVERYONE who jumps aboard the bullet train destined for the stage with the red dot.

My role as a mindset coach is to help the speakers shake their jitters and ensure they leave an impactful legacy. My "secret" to getting them there is to help them harness their strength of character and unwavering passion. Here are four key keys I have them reflect on over the months leading up to the event:

1. WHY. I first ask them to remember WHY they wanted to share their "BIG IDEA." I then have them deeply anchor into *that* feeling of "WHY" and pull it out whenever they feel stressed or overwhelmed.

2. Visualize. I also have them visualize themselves on the day of the talk and see themselves walking off the stage to a standing ovation. I ask them how they feel at that moment. I have them bask in the glory of knowing that they did everything they could do to "nail their talk." I ask them to think about what they must do *now* to achieve that feeling then.

3. Think BIG. Next, I ask them to think about the month beyond the big day and have them start planning for what they'll do to fill the void and emptiness that often comes on the other side of the standing ovation. This will help them properly recover and fill their *after TEDx life* with their "next" epic adventures.

4. Reflection. Finally, the month before they give their talk, I have them go back and visualize the day they received the email that they landed their big talk. I have them look at how far they've come over those months and applaud themselves for the exponential growth they achieved along the way.

I've found that the speakers' wise self-reflection during these simple exercises helps them clear away their jitters and sets them up for their brave and brilliant step onto the red dot.

How to have such a strong physicality that people can't take their eyes off you | Lisa Pezik, Physicality Trainer for TEDxHuntingtonBeach

I've learned the only person you're competing against is you. The only person who can play your part is you. Instead of trying to be what I thought the world wanted me to be. I took the courageous leap to be myself.

When it's your time to show the world what you've got, remember your ABCs:

1. Awareness. Ask yourself, "What does the audience need from me right now?" Is it connection, validation, hope, compassion, laughter, inspiration, tough love?" Start by giving it to yourself. We can't give to others what we don't give to ourselves.

2. Buoyancy. We can't look away from a body that moves free of limitations and apologies. It's not who's the loudest or never makes mistakes. Comedy, vulnerability, and real life-changing ideas are rooted in truth. We must spend time with ourselves and our thoughts to know who we are. Don't cheat on preparation and rehearsal.

3. Centering. Our breath is our engine. If you need to take a deep breath, your audience may need one, too. Those micropauses make you human. The world can wait a second while you center on yourself, your environment, and others.

Our job is to take care of the audience. Don't forget to take care of yourself. The body never lies, and we need you to live into your truth.

How to choose the best outfit for your TEDx talk | Erin Tran, Event and Speaker Director for TEDxHuntingtonBeach

When it comes to choosing an outfit, think of it as your 'legacy outfit.' Sure, it's the outfit you'll wear on the day of the live event and the audience will see you, but they are not really who it's for. Your outfit—including hair, skin, nails, accessories, etc... will become memorialized online on the TEDx YouTube channel. Wear something that is comfortable, represents who you are, and is aligned with your message.

1. What Not to Wear. Each stage is slightly different, and you want to know the boundaries before you imagine the perfect outfit and then find out it won't work. Ask your TEDx event team if there are any colors or patterns to avoid based on the lighting and background. Ask about jewelry constraints so it doesn't interfere with audio and recording equipment.

2. What to Wear. Once you know the guidelines, think about plays, concerts, or live shows you've seen – the outfits are usually loud and over the top. The stage is a distance away from the audience and somehow, the saturation gets lost both in person and on video.

You don't want to look 'faded.' I remember when my son was in the kids' theater, he wore so much red lipstick, blush, and mascara that I thought he wouldn't look like his boy role once he was on stage. I was wrong. After that first night, we DOUBLED the amount of make-up he was wearing (because it looked like he had no color to his skin). We don't want to be as loud and blingy as a singer on tour, but we do want to be our boldest selves while remaining in vibe with who we are and what we are speaking about.

3. About the footwear. Keep it aligned with the outfit. Simple and comfortable is best. You do NOT want to trip on the red dot or have your footwear detract from what you are saying!

How to leverage your TEDx talk to make an impact and create a legacy | Dr. Izdihar Jamil, Curator and Organizer for TEDxHuntingtonBeach

Once you've given your TEDx talk, it's not the end. In fact, it's just a starting point to something amazing. A lot of speakers I see stop doing anything, assuming that once they've given their talk, the book deals, business, clients, fame, and money will come to them with little to no effort. Unfortunately, that's not the case. Often, only a few hundred people view their talk, and nothing much happens. You need to leverage your TEDx talk effectively to make an impact and create a legacy. Here's how:

1. Share Your Journey. Share your journey throughout the TEDx process. This creates a connection with the audience and plants the seeds for them to view your talk and share it. Let people in on the behind-the-scenes moments, the challenges you faced, and the lessons you learned. This transparency builds a bond with your audience, making them more invested in your message.

2. Highlight Key Points. Once your talk is delivered, create multiple 30 to 60 second reels to highlight the key points from your talk. Share these on your social media every week for 12 months. Give value to your audience consistently. These snippets keep your message alive and

91

reach a wider audience. You'll thank me for the unimaginable outcomes as more people engage with your ideas and share them.

3. Transform Your Talk. Leverage your talk further by transforming it into other formats. Write a book based on your talk, create a podcast, and use it during your speeches. Don't let your idea die. Transform it into tangible tools that can be spread across multiple platforms. This keeps your message alive and helps it reach diverse audiences, creating a lasting impact and a legacy.

Your TEDx talk is just the beginning. Share your journey, consistently highlight key points, and transform your talk into various formats to make a lasting impact. Remember, the effort you put in after your talk is what will truly create a legacy.

How to calm your nerves and give the best TEDx talk | The TEDxHuntingtonBeach Team

Stepping into the limelight of the coveted red dot can often be daunting and scary. There are usually a lot of nerves as it's the pinnacle of months and perhaps years of hard work. We wanted to share with you four practical tips to calm your nerves.

Tip #1. Once you memorize your speech, use your phone's default voice memo app and record yourself saying your speech exactly as you will on stage. Then get out and walk and say your speech over and over while listening to it (i.e., with earbuds/headphones). This will help you with the cadence, tone, pauses, etc., and ensure that the day of, it feels natural rather than 'memorized.' It'll be so rehearsed that it won't sound rehearsed. And you won't have to worry about forgetting a line. *Shared by Erin Tran.*

Tip #2. As a speaker and performer, there's a moment where we 'wait in the wings.' We're behind the curtain as our name is announced. As a solo performer, you're alone with your thoughts and need a place for your adrenaline to go. Before each performance, I do a shake, swirl, and scoop. I shake out my whole body, then swirl my hips side to side, and lastly, I scoop my hands together from my feet to the top of my head, pulling in good energy. Use those nerves as rocket fuel. If you're nervous, it means you care! *Shared by Lisa Pezik.*

Tip #3. When the day of the event arrives, the speaker's adrenaline-fueled energy needs to be managed and paced. To help them find their "calm pacing," I teach them how to "box breathe," where they breathe in deeply for three seconds, hold their breath for 3 seconds, and gently exhale for three seconds. This technique quickly taps into their parasympathetic system so that they take complete control over their minds in the moments before, during, and after their standing ovation-worthy talk. *Shared by Laura Clancy.*

Tip #4. Just seconds before stepping on stage, I said a prayer, "God, just let me BE. Let them hear my heart. Let me touch their hearts. Help me to take care of one person so I can be grateful." Then I opened my eyes, smiled at the audience, and said my first line, "My husband, Rizal…" Take a moment to connect with the Creator to set your intention. You have only one job for the day, take care of one person, so you can be so grateful. Keep your focus on the AUDIENCE on how you can take of them as it's not about you. *Shared by Dr. Izdihar Jamil, Ph.D.*

Move with bravery even when you're scared and tap into your brilliance. You've got this, and we can't wait to hear about your success!

Best Wishes,
Izdihar, Erin, Laura, and Lisa
TEDxHuntingtonBeach 2024 Team

More info

Dr. Izdihar Jamil, Ph.D.:
https://www.izdiharjamil.com/

Erin Tran: http://erintran.com/

Laura Clancy: https://www.muffintoppled.com/

Lisa Pezik: https://www.infinitedesignhouse.com/